MIGHTY ANIMAL MIGRATIONS

A PENGUIN'S JOURNEY

David and Julie Lavender

Enslow PUBLISHING

Please visit our website, www.enslow.com. For a free color catalog of all our high-quality books, call toll free 1-800-398-2504 or fax 1-877-980-4454

Published in 2027 by
Enslow Publishing
2544 Clinton Street
Buffalo, NY 14224

Cataloging-in-Publication Data
Names: Lavender, David R., 1961-, author. | Lavender, Julie, author.
Title: A penguin's journey / by David and Julie Lavender.
Description: Buffalo, NY : Enslow Publishing, 2027. | Series: Mighty animal migrations | Includes glossary.
Identifiers: ISBN 9781978549579 (pbk.) | ISBN 9781978549586 (library bound) | ISBN 9781978549593 (ebook)
Subjects: LCSH: Emperor penguin--Migration--Juvenile literature.
Classification: LCC QL696.S473 L384 2027 | DDC 598.471568--dc23

Photo credits: Cover, p 1, Ivan Hoermann/Shutterstock.com; Calendars used throught interior, Evolvect/AdobeStock.com; p 5, Altitude Visual/Shutterstock.com; p 6, TravelMediaProduction/Shutterstock.com; p 7, Altitude Visual/Shutterstock.com; p 8, Mario_Hoppmann/Shutterstock.com; p 9, Joey_Danuphol/Shutterstock.com; p 10, AI generated; p 11, Martyna Nawrocka/Shutterstock.com; p 12, DesireBajo/Shutterstock.com; p 13, Sergey 402/Shutterstock.com; p 14, vladsilver/Shutterstock.com; p 15, Tarpan/Shutterstock.com; p 16, Shaikh sk/Shutterstock.com; p 17, Roger ARPS BPE1 CPAGB, Mario_Hoppman/Shutterstock.com; p 18, TETSU Snowdrop/Shutterstock.com; p 19, Sergey 402/Shutterstock.com; p 20, vladsilver/Shutterstock.com; p 21, Agami Photo Agency/Shutterstock.com, stylefoto24/Shutterstock.com; p 22, Francois Guerraz @Wiki; p 23, vladsilver/Shutterstock.com; p 24, Mozgova/Shutterstock.com; p 25, 27, juan68/Shutterstock.com; p 29, AI generated(Background)

Printed in China

CPSIA compliance information: Batch #CSENS27: For further information, contact Enslow Publishing, New York, New York, at 1-800-398-2504.

Table of Contents

Journey Across the Ice 4
Migration Begins 6
An Icy Walk 8
Emperor Penguin Egg 10
Survival on the Ice 12
A New Penguin Chick 14
Switching Places 16
Taking Turns 18
Penguin Chicks on Their Own 20
New Set of Feathers 22
The New Chick's First Swim 24
Harsh, Icy Journey 26
A Penguin Migration Map 28
Glossary 30
Fact Check 31
Further Reading 31
Index 32
About the Authors 32

Journey Across the Ice

Millions of animals migrate to search for food, better climate, or a safe place to birth their young. Many of those journeys take place over hundreds or thousands of miles.

Some animals migrate over land. Some swim long distances. Some migrate over both land and water.

Emperor penguins migrate 60 to 100 miles (97 to 160 km) across ice to birth their chicks. The distance may seem small compared to other migrations. But the journey through freezing temperatures and high winds is very dangerous.

Penguin Press Release

Emperor penguins are the only penguins to lay eggs and raise chicks on ice in Antarctica. Emperor penguins spend their entire lives on the ice or in the surrounding waters.

Migration Begins

Early one morning in April, an emperor penguin leaps from the waters of Weddell Sea onto the icy shelf of Antarctica. Another penguin does the same. Then, another and another.

The emperor penguin migration begins. For six days, males and females march across the ice. They search in large groups for thick, sturdy ice.

Temperatures are well below freezing. Bitter, cold winds blow at 60 miles (97 km) per hour.

Penguin Press Release

Emperor penguins are the largest of all penguins. They are about as tall as most third graders! Emperor penguins and Adélie penguins live only on Antarctica. Other penguin species, such as the chinstrap, macaroni, gentoo, rockhopper, king, and Magellanic penguins, live around Antarctica.

An Icy Walk

The long journey across 75 miles (121 km) ends. Thousands of male and female emperor penguins gather on ice that is strong enough to hold them.

Now, the **courtship** begins. Penguins wander around the ice, calling and singing. They are looking for a mate. Their heads bow and swing. They strut across the ice.

Once pairs form, they often face each other and bow in sync. They waddle across the ice together. The male and female mate.

Penguin Press Release

Emperor penguins return to the same location year after year. **Instinct** guides their way. They also use the position of the sun and stars to help them.

Emperor Penguin Egg

Soon, the female penguin lays an egg. She moves the egg. Slowly. Carefully. The egg is fragile. But she must hurry. The egg could freeze quickly. The chick inside would die.

She places the egg on top of her mate's feet. He covers it with his **brood pouch**. This layer of feathered skin keeps the egg warm and cozy.

The penguins have been without food for two months. The female leaves her mate and makes the long walk back to the sea to find food.

Penguin Press Release

Since Antarctica is south of the equator, its seasons are opposite of places north of the equator. Scientists consider Antarctica to have only two seasons: summer and winter. Summer lasts from late October through early March, and winter goes from March to October.

Survival on the Ice

The male penguin **incubates** the egg for the next 65 days. He can't drop or leave the egg, even for a second. If he does, it might crack or freeze. He sleeps standing up. He doesn't eat. He depends on fat reserves in his body to survive.

The weather is harsh. The days get colder and colder. The wind blows. Winter storms come. Hurricane-force winds whip across the ice at 120 miles (193 km) per hour.

The male penguins gather close in a huddle. Standing together helps them stay warm by sharing body heat.

Penguin Press Release

When penguins huddle in a tight group, the penguins on the outside feel the cold and wind the most. The penguins keep moving and changing places so others can have a turn in the middle, the warmest spot.

A New Penguin Chick

In the middle of a blizzard in late August, an emperor penguin chick hatches. Lots of penguin chicks hatch within days of each other. Some of the mother penguins have returned from the sea, but not all of them.

The penguin chick stays tucked inside his father's brood pouch. He's born with just a thin layer of **down**. It is too thin to keep him warm.

His mother hasn't made it back from **foraging** for food in the sea. The male penguin feeds the chick some milk. He produces the nutrient-rich milk in a special place in his throat.

leopard seal

Penguin Press Release

Sadly, some female penguins will not return to their chicks. Some starve, and some are eaten by leopard seals. Male penguins face the same challenges. Sometimes, penguin chicks can't survive a winter storm, especially if the storm breaks apart the ice. The chicks might drown.

Switching Places

The male penguin hears the call of his mate. He answers in return. The mother **regurgitates** food from her stomach to feed her chick. Mushy, half-chewed fish is perfect for the small penguin. She keeps the chick warm in her brood pouch.

Now, it's the male penguin's turn to walk across the ice back to open waters. He hasn't eaten in four months.

The mother penguin feeds and cares for the chick. The young penguin spends time outside the brood pouch now.

Taking Turns

The male penguin returns from feeding in the open waters of Weddell Sea. The mother and father penguin take turns caring for the chick.

While the male penguin watches the chick and feeds him chewed-up food from his stomach, the female penguin swims and hunts. Then, they switch jobs.

The ice begins to melt from the edges with summer approaching. Open water is not as far away now.

Penguin Chicks on Their Own

The mother and father penguin leave at the same time now to search for food. They'll continue to feed the chick for several more weeks.

The penguin chick spends most of his time huddling with other chicks. They form a tight group to stay warm. Penguin chicks are safer in numbers too.

Suddenly, a large shadow looms. A flock of predatory birds swoops down to snatch a small penguin. The hatchlings huddle tighter.

southern giant petrel

south polar skua

Penguin Press Release

While in the water, emperor penguins face predators like leopard seals and killer whales. On the ice, adult emperor penguins do not have predators. However, penguin chicks are easily taken as prey by birds like south polar skuas and southern giant petrels.

New Set of Feathers

The young chick begins to **molt**. His down is replaced with waterproof feathers. It will take a little more than a month for all of the feathers to grow.

The penguin chick continues to huddle with other chicks for warmth. The mother and father penguins do not feed the young chick once he starts molting.

Adult male and female penguins prepare to molt and head back to sea to forage. They need to build up their fat reserves for another winter and to prepare for next year's chicks. Thousands of young chicks are left on the ice until their molting is complete.

Penguin Press Release

Emperor penguins reach sexual maturity at three years old. Most won't start breeding until they are six. They usually lay one egg each year. Emperor penguins can live for 20 years. That's a lot of penguin offspring!

The New Chick's First Swim

The emperor chick is finally ready to make his way to the open water. Along with other new chicks, he walks to the edge of the ice. He leaps into the water, moves his flippers, and paddles his feet.

He swims under the ice and gobbles up krill. He slurps small fish. He dives deeper and nibbles on squid.

With lots of practice, he'll dive deep under water. He can stay under for up to 20 minutes. He'll stay at sea until it's his turn to migrate across the ice to mate and care for his own chick.

JANUARY √

to

MARCH √

Harsh, Icy Journey

The largest penguins in the world make an epic, icy journey to breed and raise their young. Emperor penguins leave the open waters surrounding Antarctica. They migrate up to 100 miles (160 km) across ice to reach their breeding location. They'll mate, lay eggs, and raise their chicks.

Unlike some animals, both emperor penguin parents care for and feed their young. The male takes the first duty. The female takes the second duty. Then, they both take turns feeding the chicks.

The conditions are harsh and dangerous, with freezing temperatures and strong winds. But these penguins survive and thrive.

A Penguin Migration Map

1. Emperor penguins leave the open sea and migrate 60 to 100 miles (97 to 160 km) to the breeding location.
2. Penguins pair up after a time of courtship. The penguins mate.
3. Male penguins incubate eggs. Female penguins go back to sea to feed.
4. Penguin chicks hatch. Male penguins keep the chick warm in their brood pouch. Females return from feeding.
5. Male penguins return to sea to feed. Then, both parents take turns foraging for food and feeding chicks.
6. Penguin chicks huddle together to stay warm while adults feed and get ready to leave breeding location.
7. Penguin chicks molt and ice breaks up. The adults leave to feed in the open sea.
8. When molting is complete, penguin chicks head to sea to forage for food.

JAN-MARCH
Feeding
Weddell Sea
Marching
APRIL
Females go off to feed
Males go off to feed
Molting
DEC
Mating
MAY
Females return
Incubating
JUNE-JULY
Hatching
AUGUST
Feeding
SEPT-OCT
Huddling
OCT-NOV
Antarctica

Glossary

brood pouch (brood pouch): a special pocket on an animal's body where eggs are kept safe and warm

courtship (KORT-ship): special actions or displays adult animals do to attract a mate

down (doun): a layer of soft, fluffy feathers that keep a chick warm

foraging (FOR-uh-jing): searching for food

incubates (ING-kyuh-bates): keeping eggs warm against the body until it is time for them to hatch

instinct (IN-stingkt): behavior that is natural and not learned

molt (mohlt): when an animal sheds its outer covering of fur, feathers, or skin

regurgitates (ri-GUR-juh-tates): to vomit up partially digested food

Fact Check

1. The male emperor penguin keeps its egg on top of its ____.
   a. head b. feet c. tail

2. Emperor penguins _________ as they migrate to their breeding place.
   a. fly b. swim c. walk

3. The largest of all penguin species is the ______________.
   a. emperor b. macaroni c. rockhopper

Answers: 1. b, 2. c, 3. a

Further Reading

Bergman, Charles. *Every Penguin in the World: A Quest to See Them All*. Sasquatch Books, 2020.

deNapoli, Dyan. *All About Penguins: Discover Life on Land and in the Sea*. Callisto Kids, 2020.

Gieseke, Tyler. *Migration Cycles*. ABDO, 2023.

On the Internet

10 Facts About Emperor Penguins
www.natgeokids.com/nz/discover/animals/birds/emperor-penguins/
Learn 10 facts about these Antarctica birds and see cool pictures too.

Emperor Penguin
https://kids.nationalgeographic.com/animals/birds/facts/emperor-penguin
Learn the stats about emperor penguins, more facts and trivia, and watch a cool video about penguin parents.

Publisher's note to educators and parents: Our editors have carefully reviewed these websites to ensure that they are suitable for students. Many websites change frequently, however, and we cannot guarantee that a site's future contents will continue to meet our high standards of quality and educational value. Be advised that students should be closely supervised whenever they access the internet.

Index

Antarctica 4, 6, 7, 11, 26, 29

egg 4, 10, 12, 23, 26, 28

feathers 22

flippers 24

hatchling 20

leopard seal 15, 21

migration 6, 28, 29

predators 15, 20, 21

About the Authors

David and Julie Lavender have never seen penguins in the wild, but have loved learning about them at zoos, aquariums, and other places. The authors think they are awesomely cool! In fact, David and Julie love learning about all kinds of animals. They enjoy writing books that help kids learn to love and appreciate nature and wildlife too. They've written lots of nonfiction books, like this migration series, and some fiction ones like *A Gingerbread House*. The Lavenders have four adult children and three grandkids.